INDIA

R.L. Van

Big Buddy Books
An Imprint of Abdo Publishing
abdobooks.com

abdobooks.com

Published by Abdo Publishing, a division of ABDO, PO Box 398166, Minneapolis, Minnesota 55439.
Copyright © 2023 by Abdo Consulting Group, Inc. International copyrights reserved in all countries. No part of this book may be reproduced in any form without written permission from the publisher. Big Buddy Books™ is a trademark and logo of Abdo Publishing.

Printed in the United States of America, North Mankato, Minnesota
102022
012023

Design: Emily O'Malley, Mighty Media, Inc.
Production: Mighty Media, Inc.
Editor: Jessica Rusick
Cover Photograph: Olena Tur/Shutterstock Images
Interior Photographs: Anastasiia Guseva/Shutterstock Images, p. 30 (flag); andrijosef/Shutterstock Images, p. 26 (left); AP Images, p. 11; Catalin Lazar/Shutterstock Images, p. 27 (top left); Debatosh Sengupta/Flickr, p. 29 (top); Denis.Vostrikov/Shutterstock Images, p. 30 (currency); Dhaval R Prajapati/Shutterstock Images, p. 13; Dinodia Photos/Wikimedia Commons, p. 21; Dreame Walker/Shutterstock Images, p. 23; Emrah C. Adalioglu/Shutterstock Images, p. 27 (top right); Filip Bjorkman/Shutterstock Images, p. 7 (map); lukulo/ iStockphoto, pp. 5 (compass), 7 (compass); Nuamfolio/Shutterstock Images, p. 26 (right); OPIS Zagreb/ Shutterstock Images, p. 25; Pyty/Shutterstock Images, p. 5 (map); Roop_Dey/Shutterstock Images, p. 6 (bottom); saiko3p/Shutterstock Images, p. 6 (middle); Sean Hsu/Shutterstock Images, p. 6 (top); Shutterstock Images, pp. 15, 17, 19; Wikimedia Commons, pp. 9, 28 (both); WorldStockStudio/Shutterstock Images, p. 27 (bottom); YashSD/Shutterstock Images, p. 29 (bottom)
Design Elements: Mighty Media, Inc.
Country population and area figures taken from the CIA World Factbook

Library of Congress Control Number: 2022940523

Publisher's Cataloging-in-Publication Data
Names: Van, R.L., author.
Title: India / by R.L. Van
Description: Minneapolis, Minnesota : Abdo Publishing, 2023 | Series: Countries | Includes online resources and index.
Identifiers: ISBN 9781532199639 (lib. bdg.) | ISBN 9781098274832 (ebook)
Subjects: LCSH: India--Juvenile literature. | Asia--Juvenile literature. | India--History--Juvenile literature. | Geography--Juvenile literature.
Classification: DDC 954--dc23

CONTENTS

PASSPORT TO INDIA

India is a country in South Asia. It borders six countries and the Indian Ocean. It has the second-highest population in the world. More than 1.3 billion people live there.

Hindi and English are India's official languages. But hundreds of different languages are spoken there.

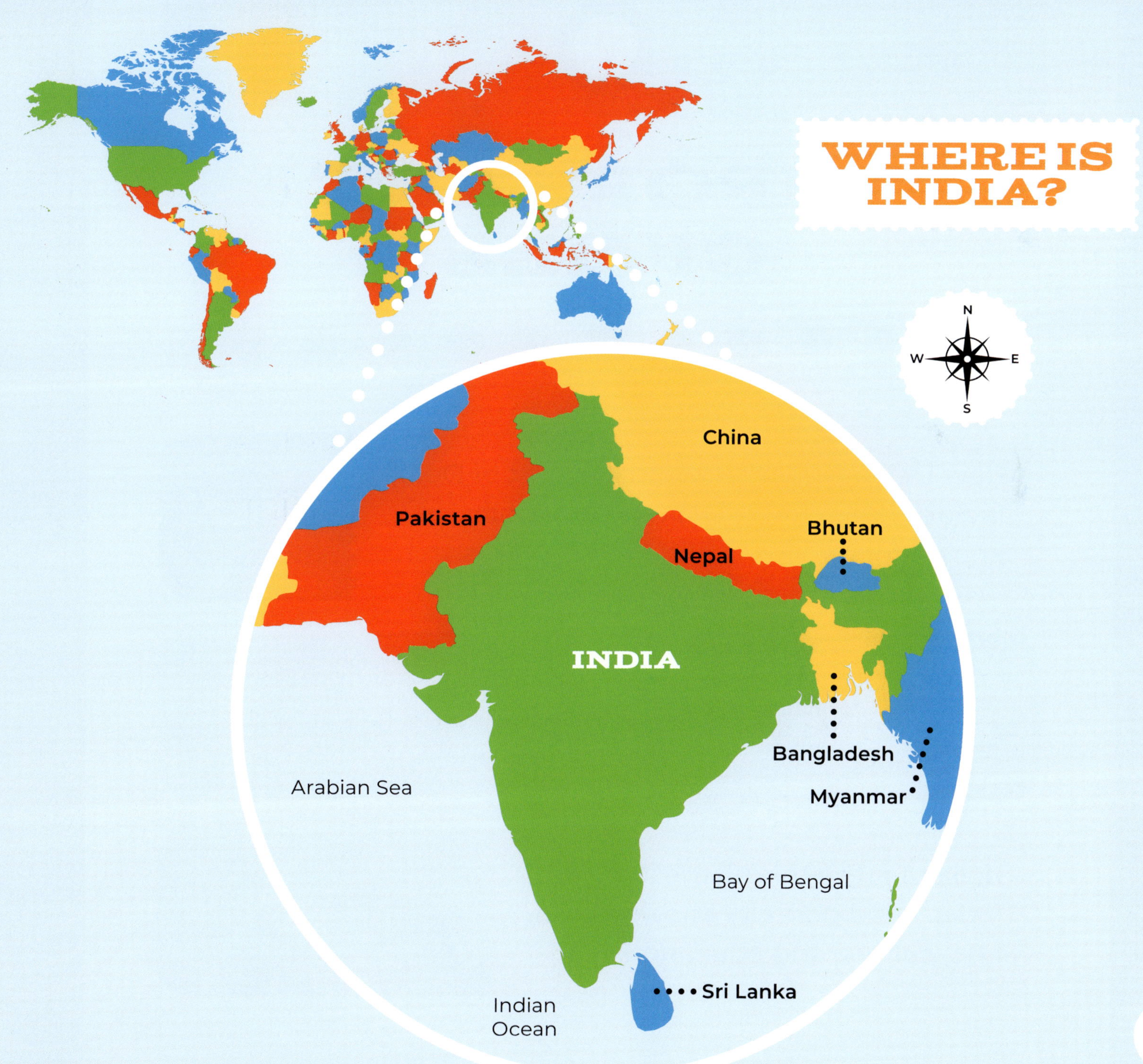

WHERE IS INDIA?
China
Pakistan
Bhutan
Nepal
INDIA
Arabian Sea
Bangladesh
Myanmar
Bay of Bengal
Sri Lanka
Indian Ocean
N
W
E
S

IMPORTANT CITIES

New Delhi is India's **capital**. It is part of Delhi, India's largest **metropolitan area**. Delhi is known for its history and marketplaces.

Mumbai is India's second-largest metropolitan area. It is a center of business and entertainment.

Kolkata is the third-largest city in India. It is a port city known for its arts, culture, and education.

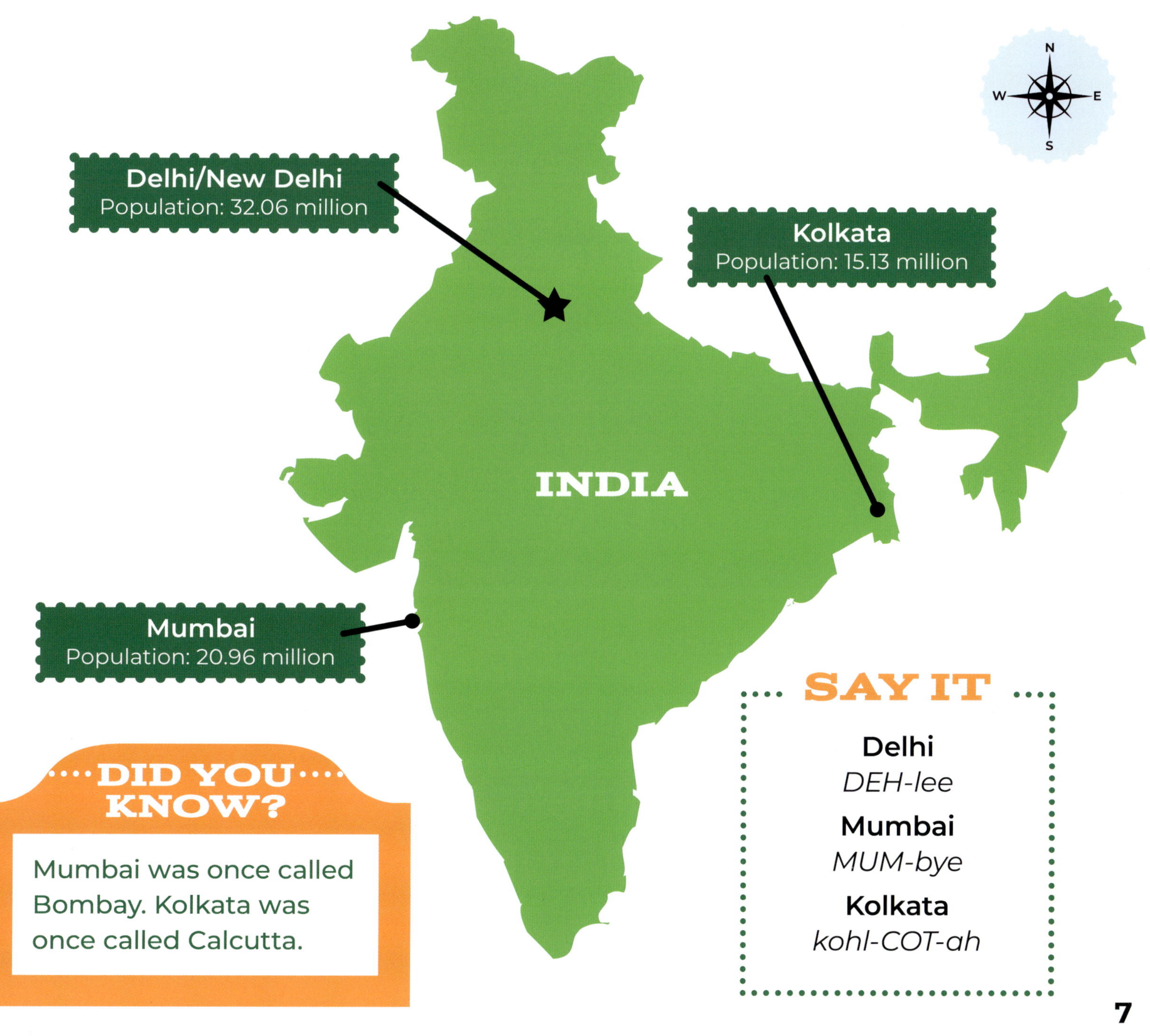

DID YOU KNOW?

Mumbai was once called Bombay. Kolkata was once called Calcutta.

SAY IT

Delhi
DEH-lee

Mumbai
MUM-bye

Kolkata
kohl-COT-ah

INDIA IN HISTORY

India's first **civilization** started more than 4,000 years ago in the Indus Valley. Over the years, many groups ruled India. It became known as a rich country because of its fabrics, gold, and spices. In the late 1400s, Europeans arrived in India.

The Indus Valley
Civilization is also
known as the
Harappan Civilization.

9

The British East India Company began ruling India in the 1750s. Great Britain took over in 1858. India fought back and won independence in 1947.

Today, many people in India live in poverty. There is also conflict and **corruption**. But India's people are working to improve these situations.

Jawaharlal Nehru (*saluting*) became the first prime minister of an independent India in August 1947.

AN IMPORTANT SYMBOL

India's flag was adopted in 1947. It has orange, white, and green stripes. Its center wheel is called a chakra.

India is a **federal parliamentary republic**. The president is head of state. The prime minister is head of government. The two houses of parliament make laws.

The orange color on
India's flag is also called
saffron. It stands for
courage and sacrifice.

ACROSS THE LAND

India has forests, rivers, beaches, and deserts. The Himalaya mountains are in the north.

Bengal tigers, leopards, monkeys, and elephants live in India. Lotuses, mangoes, teak, and bamboo grow there.

Jim Corbett National Park is in northern India. It is home to elephant herds.

EARNING A LIVING

India's biggest **employer** is Indian Railways. Some Indian people work in factories. Others work for software companies.

India's **natural resources** include iron ore, copper, coal, and petroleum. Farmers produce wheat, chickpeas, sugarcane, cotton, and tea.

Indian Railways employs more than 1 million people.

LIFE IN INDIA

Indian people often eat grains and vegetables with many spices. Milk, tea, and coffee are popular drinks.

Indian people like **cricket**, field hockey, and soccer. Many enjoy movies and music from **Bollywood**. Most Indian people practice **Hinduism**.

SAY IT

Hinduism
HIN-doo-ih-zuhm

Musicians in Mumbai perform during Gudhi Padwa, a Hindu New Year celebration.

FAMOUS FACES

Mohandas Gandhi was born in Porbandar, India, in 1869. Many consider him the father of India. That's because he helped free the country from British rule. Gandhi fought for Indian rights in peaceful ways. He was killed in 1948. He is remembered for his work.

Gandhi's birthday is
a national holiday in
India. It is celebrated
on October 2.

Priyanka Chopra was born in Jamshedpur, India. In 2000, she won the Miss World pageant. She began acting shortly after. She acts in both American and **Bollywood** movies and TV shows. Chopra has won many awards. She also does work to help Indian children access health care and education.

Priyanka Chopra is married to singer Nick Jonas. In 2022, the couple welcomed a daughter, Malti.

A GREAT COUNTRY

India is known for its long history and unique culture. The people and places of India help make the world a more interesting place.

The Himalayas cross
northeastern India.
The range has jungles
and icy peaks.

25

If you ever visit India, here are some places to go and things to do!

EXPLORE

Spot tigers at India's Nagarahole National Park.

DISCOVER

See both Mount Everest and Mount Kanchenjunga from Tiger Hill. They are the highest and third-highest mountains in the world.

SEE

Visit the city of Agra to see the Taj Mahal. It took more than 20,000 workers to build it!

CELEBRATE

Visit Jaipur for Holi, the Festival of Colors, and get covered in bright colors!

SWIM

Take a dip in the Arabian Sea at some of the many unique beaches of Goa, such as Butterfly Beach.

TIMELINE

ABOUT 300-600

The Golden Age of India took place. There was lots of growth in the arts, sciences, and other fields.

1498

Vasco da Gama became the first European to arrive in India by sea.

1757

The British East India Company took control of Bengal. It expanded further into India over the following years.

1947

India gained its independence from Great Britain.

2007

Pratibha Patil became the
first female president of India.

2011

India won the
Cricket World Cup.

2020

Javelin thrower Neeraj Chopra
(*left*) won India's first-ever
Olympic gold medal for a
track-and-field event.

INDIA

UP CLOSE

Official Name
Bharatiya Ganarajya
(Republic of India)

Flag

Population
1,389,637,446 (2022 est.)
2nd-most-populated country

Total Area
1,269,219 square miles
(3,287,263 sq km)
7th-largest country

Official Languages
Hindi, English

Capital
New Delhi

Currency
Indian rupee

Form of Government
Federal parliamentary
republic

National Anthem
"Jana Gana Mana"
("Thou Art the Ruler
of the Minds of All
People")

GLOSSARY

Bollywood—the Indian film industry.

capital—a city where government leaders meet.

civilization—a well-organized and advanced society.

corruption—dishonest or illegal behaviors done by people in power for personal gain.

cricket—a sport where players try to bat a ball off the field and run back and forth between sets of posts called wickets to score runs. The other team tries to get them out.

employer—a person or company that pays people for their work.

federal parliamentary republic—a government in which people elect representatives to parliament, and these representatives choose a leader. The central government and the individual states and territories share power.

Hinduism—a religion practiced mainly in India. Hindus believe in many gods and goddesses and typically believe people are reborn in other forms after death. They consider certain texts, objects, and animals sacred.

metropolitan area—a large city and its surrounding cities and suburbs.

natural resources—useful and valuable supplies from nature.

ONLINE RESOURCES

To learn more about India, please visit **abdobooklinks.com** or scan this QR code. These links are routinely monitored and updated to provide the most current information available.

INDEX